ASSUMING DEFINITE SHAPE

—Alley in the Memphis *Commercial Appeal.*

Cornerstones of Freedom

The Story of

THE TEAPOT DOME SCANDAL

By Jim Hargrove

CHILDRENS PRESS®
CHICAGO

Winners of the National Charleston Championship held in
the Trianon Ballroom in Chicago, Illinois

Library of Congress Cataloging-in-Publication Data

Hargrove, Jim.

The story of the Teapot Dome scandal / by Jim Hargrove.
    p.   cm. — (Cornerstones of freedom)
  Summary: Describes the causes, events, and aftermath of
the scandal known as Teapot Dome which helped ruin the
reputation of the administration of Warren G. Harding, the
twenty-ninth president.
  ISBN 0-516-04722-1
  1. Teapot Dome Scandal, 1921-1924 — Juvenile
literature.
[1. Teapot Dome Scandal, 1921-1924.]
I. Title. II. Series.
E785.H33 1989   89-33785
973.91'4 — dc20   CIP
                                                  AC

PHOTO CREDITS

Historical Picture Service — Cover (inset),
  2, 13 (bottom), 19, 21 (right), 24 (3 photos
  31 (left)
Wide World Photos — 4, 6, 9, 11 (inset), 17
  (left), 27 (both photos), 30
Wyoming State Historical Society — Cover,
  11, 32
UPI/BETTMANN NEWSPHOTOS — 8, 13
  (top middle), 17 (right), 20 (2 photos), 21
  (left), 31 (right)

During the 1920s, a scandal known as Teapot Dome helped ruin the reputation of President Warren G. Harding. Despite the determined efforts of a few politicians and businessmen to hide the facts, this tempest about a teapot colored American politics for a decade.

And what an amazing decade it was! The period of American history from 1920 to 1930 has been given many names, including the Roaring Twenties and the Jazz Age. The decade might also have been called the Age of Teapot Dome. This scandal began in 1921 and was finally put to rest in 1929, the very year the Roaring Twenties came to a crashing end.

Near the start of the era, in November 1920, the first commercial radio broadcast was made by station KDKA in Pittsburgh. By the end of the 1920s, when the last bits of news about the scandal were learned, most American homes owned at least one radio. By the millions, Americans listened to jazz music. Dances such as the Charleston kept up with the lively new music.

For the first time, some women wore dresses short enough to expose their knees. Motion pictures also became a huge industry during the twenties. The first "talkies" appeared in 1927. And by 1929,

Cars filled parking lots such as this one at Nantasket Beach, Massachusetts.

yearly theater attendance approached six billion in
the United States alone.

The automobile also came of age during the Roaring Twenties. In 1920, there were about eight million registered automobiles in America. Nine years
later, the number had nearly tripled, to twenty-
three million. What many Americans wanted most
was a car. And what the automobile engines needed
most was gasoline, the light, almost clear liquid produced from crude oil. Appropriately enough, oil and
the fortunes that could be made from it were what
the Teapot Dome scandal was all about.

The words *Teapot Dome* refer not to a teapot but to an oil field in Wyoming, near the city of Casper. At Teapot Dome, geologists found vast quantities of crude oil under a layer of rock that bulged upward like a huge dome.

As early as 1910, the U.S. Congress realized that oil was important not only to America's citizens but to its armed forces as well. To make sure that oil would be available for the huge ships of the U.S. Navy, Congress authorized the government to take over two large oil fields in California. Both were to be held in reserve for the navy. In 1915, President Woodrow Wilson added the Teapot Dome, calling it Naval Oil Reserve Number Three.

Not everyone thought the huge oil fields on public land should be left as reserves. A number of businessmen felt they should have the right to lease the land and extract the oil for profit, paying a royalty to the government. Some people, including a few of President Wilson's top advisers, felt that it was dangerous to leave the oil underground. Oil wells had been sunk on private lands near the reserves, they pointed out. Nearby wells might drain oil supposedly protected in the reserves.

In the last years of Wilson's administration, a

squabble broke out in his cabinet over the best ways to manage the oil reserves. Finally, in 1920, Secretary of the Navy Josephus Daniels was put in charge of the fields. The 1920 congressional bill instructed him to "conserve, develop, use and operate" the three oil reserves in the best interests of the navy and national defense.

On March 4 of the following year, 1921, Warren G. Harding was sworn in as America's twenty-ninth president. Like any incoming president, Harding began to choose people, many of whom he had known for years, to fill top-level government jobs. Edwin Denby, who had earlier served as a congressman

President Warren G. Harding with his wife Florence

President Harding and his cabinet: Seated from left to right: Secretary of War John W. Weeks; Secretary of the Treasury Andrew W. Mellon; Secretary of State Charles E. Hughes; President Warren G. Harding; Vice President Calvin Coolidge; Secretary of the Navy Edwin Denby. Standing from left to right: Secretary of the Interior Albert B. Fall; Postmaster General Will H. Hays; Attorney General Harry M. Daugherty; Secretary of Agriculture Henry C. Wallace; Secretary of Commerce Herbert Hoover; Secretary of Labor James J. Davis

from Michigan, became the new secretary of the navy. Harry M. Daugherty, an Ohio lawyer who had been Harding's campaign manager, became the U.S. attorney general.

Another old friend of the president, a rancher who had served as a U.S. senator from New Mexico, was Albert B. Fall. Although the president had planned to make him secretary of state, Fall had other ideas. Harding bowed to his old friend's wishes and named Fall secretary of the interior. Among other responsibilities, the secretary of the interior oversees public lands owned by the federal government.

Soon after Harding's cabinet was sworn in, Secretary Fall persuaded the president to transfer control of the oil reserves from the navy to the Department of the Interior. Harding issued an executive order to that effect on May 31, 1921. Oddly, the order was not published, nor was a printed copy of it stored at the State Department, the usual custom.

Despite efforts at secrecy, the transfer was soon noticed and criticized. Wisconsin Senator Robert La Follette spoke in the Senate opposing the move. The new secretary of the navy, Edwin Denby, wrote a letter to Harding objecting to the transfer, but the letter allegedly disappeared before arriving at the White House.

Almost immediately, Interior Secretary Fall signed secret contracts with two wealthy businessmen allowing them to drill for oil on two of the three government reserves. Elk Hills, part of one of the California oil fields, was thus leased to Edward L. Doheny, the head of the Pan-American Petroleum Company. Teapot Dome was leased to Harry F. Sinclair's Mammoth Oil Company.

The contracts were illegal in at least two ways. First, Secretary Fall signed them secretly, without asking for bids from other oil firms. Most government contracts are required by law to be awarded to companies that compete with one another to complete a job for the least amount of money. By awarding contracts to the lowest bidder, the government often can save many tax dollars.

The contract Fall signed with Edward Doheny called for the Pan-American Petroleum Company to store as government reserves about 16 percent of the oil taken from Elk Hills. The agreement with Harry Sinclair, allowing his company to drill at Teapot Dome, was more complex. In very rough terms, it reserved a similar percentage of petroleum for the government. Had competitive bids been required in both cases, the government would certainly have kept a far higher portion of the oil.

Secretary of the Interior Albert Fall allowed Harry F. Sinclair and the Mammoth Oil Company to drill for oil at Teapot Dome.

The contracts were illegal for a second reason. Although it was not proved until much later, Secretary Fall accepted "gifts and loans" of more than four hundred thousand dollars—a bribe—for his actions. At the time, however, only people living around Three Rivers, New Mexico, noted how Fall's finances had suddenly, and dramatically, improved. At about the time he approved the secret contracts, Fall purchased more land for his ranch, acquired additional cattle, and made other substantial improvements on his New Mexico property. He also paid off a number of old debts.

For some months, few people realized that Albert Fall had committed a serious crime. But a growing number of Washington insiders knew that some members of the Harding administration participated in illegal activities.

The Roaring Twenties were part of the Prohibition Era. On January 16, 1920, the Eighteenth Amendment of the U.S. Constitution became effective. That amendment prohibited the manufacture, sale, and transportation of alcoholic beverages throughout the United States. Nevertheless, a sizable minority of Americans continued to drink alcohol. They did so throughout the Prohibition Era,

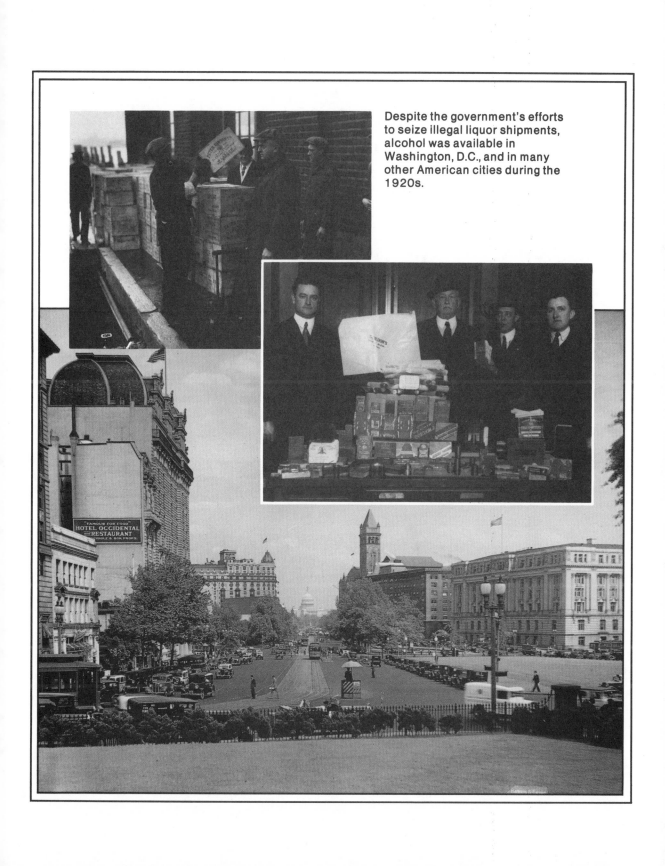

Despite the government's efforts to seize illegal liquor shipments, alcohol was available in Washington, D.C., and in many other American cities during the 1920s.

which lasted until 1933, when the Eighteenth Amendment was repealed.

Soon after the amendment was passed, illegal bars, often called speakeasies, began popping up in many different cities. One of the Washington establishments, a kind of private club for politicians and their friends, was at 1625 K Street. Rented by a member of Attorney General Harry M. Daugherty's staff, it was known as the "little green house." A number of workers from the Harding administration visited the little house on K Street. So did gangsters, drug dealers, gamblers, and party girls. Among other things, informal licenses for the production of bootleg liquor were bought and sold there.

For his part, President Harding seldom, if ever, entered the notorious K Street house. Instead, he occasionally went to a similar speakeasy on H Street, which was rented by a wealthy friend. Aside from his desire to drink illegally made alcohol, Harding was largely unaware of the growing corruption around him. But his White House life-style took some visitors by surprise. He frequently played in late-night poker games, his card table surrounded by a dizzying assortment of liquor bottles, and the White House air thick with tobacco smoke.

By spring 1922, the illegal activities of Secretary Albert Fall began to unravel. A number of private citizens interested in preserving America's natural resources began informal investigations. One was Gifford Pinchot, a former chief of the U.S. Division of Forestry (now called the Forest Service) and for many years a professor of forestry at Yale University. Another was Harry A. Slattery, a Washington lawyer who had once worked for Pinchot and shared his love of the conservation movement.

During the early stages of the investigation, Pinchot ran a campaign to become the governor of Pennsylvania. This campaign left him little time to investigate the activities of Secretary Fall. But he encouraged his friend Harry Slattery to continue.

Slattery began by contacting Wisconsin Senator Robert La Follette. Nearly a year earlier, La Follette had publicly criticized Harding's transfer of the oil reserves from the navy to the Department of the Interior. With some difficulty, La Follette acquired a typed copy of President Harding's unpublished executive order authorizing the transfer. He promptly decided that it was illegal. At Slattery's urging, La Follette considered calling for a full congressional investigation into the matter.

Sensing trouble, Secretary Fall decided to reveal some aspects of his secret deals. On April 7, 1922, he announced that, because the California reserve was in danger of being drained by nearby wells, he had authorized limited drilling at Elk Hills. He neglected to mention the Teapot Dome deal.

One week later, a front-page story in *The Wall Street Journal* reported that Teapot Dome had been leased to the Mammoth Oil Company. A week after that, on April 21, La Follette called for a Senate investigation.

Like President Harding, Senator La Follette was a Republican, but his views often clashed with those of other Republicans. Many Republican senators felt that La Follette was giving ammunition to the Democrats, who generally opposed the Harding administration. Eventually, however, his resolution to investigate the oil leases passed the Senate by a vote of fifty-eight to nothing. Thirty-nine Republican senators voted in favor of examining their own party's administration.

The Senate Committee on Public Lands and Surveys was in charge of the investigation. La Follette gave all the evidence he had gathered against Secretary Fall to committee member Thomas J. Walsh,

Senator Thomas J. Walsh (left), a Montana Democrat, worked with Senator Robert La Follette (above), a Wisconsin Republican, to uncover the truth about the oil leases.

Democratic senator from Montana. Surprisingly, while a number of newspapers across the country bitterly complained over the delays, the committee held no formal hearings for a year and a half.

In the meantime, however, the story continued to unfold. In June 1922, Secretary Fall sent Senator Walsh more than five thousand pages of documents related to what was now being called the Teapot Dome scandal. With the many documents was a letter, signed by President Harding, noting that the oil-field leases had been approved personally by the president. Most historians doubt that Harding knew about the leases before Fall signed them. Some believe that President Harding never even read the letter he signed.

At Interior Secretary Fall's urging, President Harding put the full weight of the presidency on the shaky position that the leases were legal. But the scandal refused to go away. On December 15, 1922, *The Wall Street Journal* reported that Edward Doheny's Pan-American Petroleum Company had been awarded new leases on the Elk Hills reserve in California. Eventually it was discovered that Doheny had acquired control of the entire field.

Just over two weeks later, on January 2, 1923, the White House announced that Interior Secretary Albert B. Fall was resigning, effective March 4. The statement said that Fall needed to spend more time on his New Mexico ranch and his other business. This was remarkable, because the ranch clearly became more and more prosperous the longer Fall stayed in Washington. Attorney General Harry M. Daugherty insisted that Fall was under no suspicions of wrongdoing.

Throughout the first half of 1923, the Senate Committee on Public Lands and Surveys continued its investigation at a snail's pace and without formal hearings. A few experts were asked to submit reports. A few scientists were sent to Teapot Dome to determine whether the oil was in danger of leaking into commercial wells.

President Harding and his wife leave Washington on a cross-country train trip.

As summer approached, there were growing rumors about other scandals in the Harding administration. The Justice Department, under Harry M. Daugherty, was said to be largely corrupt. One of Daugherty's assistants died, either a suicide or a murder victim. Although President Harding remained popular with the majority of Americans, there were growing rumors about his drunkenness and extramarital affairs. Partly to escape the Washington rumor mills, the President began a cross-country train trip on June 20, 1923.

The president's train traveled all the way to Alaska and then headed south. On July 28, President Harding suffered an apparent heart attack in San Francisco. Although he seemed to be recovering, he died suddenly four days later. Vice President Calvin Coolidge became the new president of the United States.

Warren and Florence Harding

Despite the rumors of corruption and personal misbehavior surrounding him, Warren G. Harding died as one of the most popular presidents in American history. Three million people gathered along the railroad tracks to watch his funeral train move eastward. But in a matter of months, his reputation was completely destroyed.

Two rumors, both almost certainly untrue, began immediately. One was that Harding had committed suicide to avoid the scandals beginning to catch up with him. The other was that his strong-willed wife, Florence, had poisoned him for the same reason. Florence herself literally fanned the flames of controversy when she gathered up and burned all the

President Calvin Coolidge (left) had to deal with the scandals caused by corrupt government officials. Political cartoons (above) made the public aware of the illegal agreements.

president's letters and notes she could find immediately after his burial.

The same year that he died, it was discovered that one of Harding's poker buddies, in charge of the Veterans Administration, had robbed the nation of millions of dollars. A lawyer working for the VA killed himself. It was soon learned that Harry Daugherty's Department of Justice routinely sold "licenses" to make illegal liquor. Bootleggers caught without the proper license could escape jail if they offered large enough bribes. Considerable evidence arose indicating that Harding's brother-in-law, who served as Director of Federal Prisons, had allowed narcotic drugs to be sold to prisoners.

The scandals that came to light seemed to be without end. The dead president's former secretary, Nan Britton, claimed that Harding had fathered her illegitimate daughter. In 1927 she published a very convincing book, called *The President's Daughter*, in an attempt to prove it. And, of course, there was Teapot Dome, the scandal that just grew and grew.

At 10:00 A.M. on October 22, 1923, the long-awaited Senate hearings on Teapot Dome finally began. Reed Smoot, a Republican senator from Utah, was the committee chairman. However, he had little interest in investigating a scandal in a Republican administration. The real investigation was led by Senator Thomas J. Walsh from Montana. The effort required considerable courage.

Although Calvin Coolidge was the nation's new president, he kept most members of the Harding administration in place. Therefore, a number of Harding's dishonest friends, including Attorney General Harry M. Daugherty, remained in office. Among Daugherty's responsibilities was overseeing the conduct of the Bureau of Investigation (later reorganized and called the FBI). The Bureau conducted a shameful reign of terror against congressional critics of Teapot Dome, especially Senator Walsh.

Bureau of Investigation agents burglarized the offices of several senators, tapped their phones and read their mail, and followed them throughout Washington. Anonymous letters were sent to Senator Walsh threatening to kill him. An unidentified man grabbed Walsh's daughter on the street while she was walking with her three-year-old child and threatened to attack her if the investigation was not stopped.

Although it started slowly, the investigation was not stopped. When Senator Walsh learned about the many improvements on ex-Secretary Fall's New Mexico ranch, he decided to find out where Fall had found the money.

Fall first claimed that he had received a loan of one hundred thousand dollars from Edward McLean, a wealthy friend. But Senator Walsh eventually proved that Fall was lying. Edward Doheny, the head of the Pan-American Petroleum Company, then decided to help Fall. Doheny said that he had loaned Fall the one hundred thousand dollars. He claimed that the loan had nothing to do with the Elk Hills oil leases. He was, he had to admit, amazingly rich. A hundred thousand dollars was a small amount to loan to such a dear old friend as Secretary

Edwin Denby   Harry Daugherty and Albert Fall   Harry Sinclair

Fall. Several days later, he even produced an IOU for this amount. Oddly, he had torn off the bottom of the document, where, he said, Secretary Fall's signature had once been.

Doheny made a dogged attempt to hide the illegal circumstances of his contract with Albert Fall. But Harry Sinclair, whose Mammoth Oil Company secretly leased the land at Teapot Dome, had much more difficulty. A one-time Sinclair employee testified that he had heard Sinclair's secretary say that he had once given sixty-eight thousand dollars to the manager of Albert Fall's ranch. The secretary was called before the committee. It was all a big mix-up, the nervous secretary explained, adding that he really had said "six or eight cows." It must have been misunderstood as "sixty-eight thou."

Even President Calvin Coolidge was embarrassed by the accusations. Although he had done little to assist the widening investigation, soon enough he would have to run for election to remain in the White House. He finally decided to do something about the Teapot Dome mess.

On Sunday morning, January 27, 1924, President Coolidge issued a statement saying that he would appoint special prosecutors to try criminal suspects in the Teapot Dome case. For the first time, people outside of Harry Daugherty's Justice Department would decide whether the scandal involved criminal wrongdoing. But the wheels of American justice turned slowly. The decade was nearly over before all the criminal cases were decided.

Before government prosecutors could organize their cases, news reports of the scandal reached their highest levels. Headlines such as "Washington Awash in Dirty Oil" were featured often in the nation's newspapers. Political casualties came quickly. Secretary of the Navy Edwin Denby resigned in February 1924. On March 1, the U.S. Senate voted in favor of beginning a full-scale investigation of Attorney General Harry Daugherty, perhaps the most crooked of all the officials left over from the Harding administration. President Coolidge finally demanded his resignation, which was announced on March 28.

By May, public outcry over the scandal finally began to diminish. On May 14, 1924, the Senate Committee on Public Lands and Surveys voted to adjourn. Politicians and the people they represented turned their attention to the presidential elections scheduled for November.

During the year he served as president completing Harding's term, Calvin Coolidge said as little as possible about Teapot Dome. He was nicknamed "Silent Cal." But despite the best efforts of some Democrats, no evidence was ever found linking him to the scandal. Although some U.S. farmers were having hard times, in general the American economy was booming. Despite the oil scandal in Washington, most Americans were prosperous and happy. Coolidge easily won the November election. "The nation wanted nothing done," joked humorist Will Rogers about President Calvin Coolidge, "and he done it."

For more than four years following the 1924 election, legal battles over the oil scandal were fought in courtrooms all over America. Government prosecutors headed by Atlee Pomerene and Owen J. Roberts made strong cases against the Teapot Dome culprits. On May 28, 1925, the U.S. District Court in Los Angeles ruled that the "loan" of one hundred

WATCH YOUR STEP

Albert Fall was found guilty of accepting a bribe from Edward L. Doheny (left). The prosecuting attorneys (above) were Peyton Gordon, Owen J. Roberts, and Atlee Pomerene.

thousand dollars that oilman Edward Doheny gave to Interior Secretary Albert Fall was, in fact, a bribe. The following year, the Circuit Court of Appeals in St. Louis ordered the cancellation of the contract allowing Harry Sinclair's Mammoth Oil Company to drill wells at Teapot Dome.

Many cases went to the Supreme Court. In February 1927, the Court canceled the contract allowing Edward Doheny's Pan-American Petroleum Company to drill at the Elk Hills, California, reserve. In October, it restored full ownership of Teapot Dome to the federal government. At about the same time, President Coolidge returned control of the reserves to the navy.

Much of the damage to America's security caused by the scandal had at last been undone. But the story of Teapot Dome still had one more weird chapter, perhaps the strangest of all.

During a court case, it was learned that Harry Sinclair had come up with the cash to bribe Secretary Fall in a most unusual way. In November 1921, Sinclair held a meeting with fellow oilmen in New York City's Vanderbilt Hotel. According to one writer, the men held "a large share of the oil, above and below ground, in the Western Hemisphere." The firms represented included Sinclair's own company as well as other giant industries, including Texas Oil Company, Midwest Refining Company, Prairie Oil and Gas Company, and Standard Oil of Indiana.

The men decided to set up a phony Canadian firm, called Continental Trading Company, to buy more than thirty million barrels of oil from American companies, and then sell it back to American companies at a profit. The transaction amounted to almost exactly fifty million dollars. No oil ever moved: the entire deal was done on paper. Of course, the thousands of stockholders who invested in the American companies were robbed of profits lost to the phony Canadian firm. But each of the oilmen present in the Vanderbilt Hotel earned an instant profit of about $750,000, in some cases more.

It was finally learned that Harry Sinclair gave $304,000 of his take to Interior Secretary Albert Fall. That was how Sinclair's Mammoth Oil Company gained control of Teapot Dome. But the story doesn't end there.

Back in 1922, before the Teapot Dome scandal broke, Sinclair decided it would be wise politically to give a huge contribution to the Republican national party. Anxious not to call attention to himself, he gave $260,000 to a man named Will Hays, who had earlier served as the Republican national chairman. Hays distributed the money to a number of wealthy businessmen, who passed much of it along to the Republican party.

All of this was finally learned in 1928, when Will Hays was called to testify at another federal investigation. At the time he testified, Hays was in the early years of a long career in the motion-picture industry. It was his job to be sure that American movies depicted high standards of morality.

By 1929, the last of the criminal and civil cases growing out of Teapot Dome had been completed.

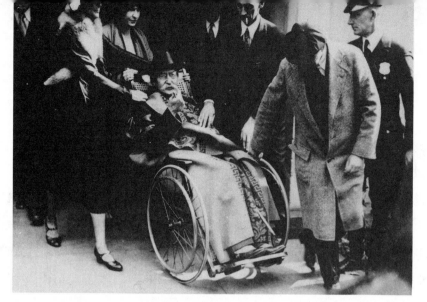

The Teapot Dome scandal ruined Albert Fall both financially and physically.

Edward L. Doheny, whose Pan-American Petroleum Company leased the Elk Hills, California, reserve, did not have to spend any time in jail. He was ordered, however, to pay back to the government about thirty-five million dollars.

Harry Sinclair, who illegally leased Teapot Dome, was not convicted of bribery. At one of his trials, however, agents working for him tampered with the jury. He was convicted of contempt of court as well as contempt of Congress and sentenced to six months in jail. He was also forced to return about twelve million dollars to the federal government. Throughout the scandal, he was hounded by blackmailers, paying them about two million dollars.

Harry Daugherty, the corrupt attorney general who saw nothing wrong with the Harding administration or Teapot Dome, was tried several times but

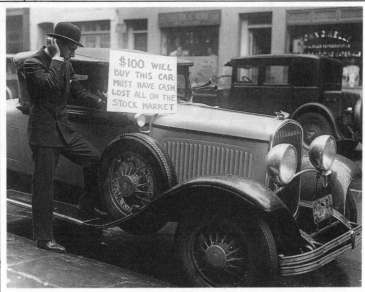

People lost money when the stock market crashed in 1929. Thousands of factories, banks, and other businesses closed. Millions of people were out of work. The good times of the Roaring Twenties were over.

never convicted. He spent twenty years in comfortable retirement.

By 1929, Albert Fall, secretary of the interior in Harding's administration, was a ruined man. His beloved ranch had been repossessed and his health seemed to be failing. On October 25, 1929, Albert Fall was found guilty of accepting a bribe and sentenced to a year in jail and a fine of one hundred thousand dollars.

The Roaring Twenties ended the same year as the Teapot Dome scandal. The New York stock market crashed in 1929, instantly removing nearly thirty billion dollars from the American economy. The Great Depression lay ahead. For Albert Fall and millions of other Americans, the good times were over.

Casper, Wyoming in the early 1920s

INDEX

About the Author

Jim Hargrove has worked as a writer and editor for more than ten years. After serving as an editorial director for three Chicago area publishers, he began a career as an independent writer, preparing a series of books for children. He has contributed to works by nearly twenty different publishers. His Childrens Press titles include biographies of Mark Twain and Richard Nixon. With his wife and daughter, he lives in a small Illinois town near the Wisconsin border.